THIS IS
NOT CHEESY!

Easy and Delicious Dairy-Free Recipes for Kids With Allergies

by KATRINA JORGENSEN

CONSULTANT
Amy Durkan MS, RDN, CDN
Nutrition Research Manager
Mount Sinai Medical Center
New York, NY

CAPSTONE PRESS
a capstone imprint

Edge Books are published by Capstone Press,
1710 Roe Crest Drive, North Mankato, Minnesota 56003
www.mycapstone.com

Library of Congress Cataloging-in-Publication Data
Cataloging-in-Publication data is on file with the Library of Congress.
ISBN 978-1-4914-8053-3 (library binding)
ISBN 978-1-4914-8058-8 (eBook PDF)

Editorial Credits
Anna Butzer, editor; Heidi Thompson, designer; Morgan Walters, media researcher;
Sarah Schuette, food stylist; Kathy McColley, production specialist

Design Elements
Shutterstock: avian, design element, Katerina Kirilova, design element, Lena Pan, design
element, Marco Govel, design element, mexrix, design element, Sabina Pittak, design
element, STILLFX, design element, swatchandsoda, design element

Photography by Capstone Studio: Karon Dubke

Editor's note:
Capstone cannot ensure that any food is allergen-free. The only way to be sure a food is
safe is to read all labels carefully, every time. Cross-contamination is also a risk for those
with food allergies. Please call food companies to make sure their manufacturing processes
avoid cross-contamination. Also, always be sure to clean hands, surfaces, and tools
before cooking.

Printed and bound in the USA.
009675F16

TABLE OF CONTENTS

WHAT IS A FOOD ALLERGY?

Our bodies are armed with immune systems. It's the immune system's job to fight infections, viruses, and invaders. Sometimes the immune system identifies a certain food as one of these invaders and attacks it. While our immune system fights, a chemical response is triggered and causes an allergic reaction. Reactions vary greatly from a mild skin irritation to having trouble breathing. Any time you feel you are having a reaction, tell an adult immediately.

The best way to avoid having an allergic reaction is to be aware of what you are eating. Be careful not to consume the allergen that affects you. If you are not sure if that allergen is in a food, ask an adult or read the ingredient label of the food container before eating. Unfortunately, allergens can sometimes be hard to identify in an ingredient list. Check out http://www.foodallergy.org for a full list of hidden dairy terms.

Avoiding dairy due to an allergy can be hard to manage, especially when it is found in so many of our favorite foods. This cookbook will take you on a culinary journey to explore many of the dishes you've had to avoid because of a dairy allergy.

Kitchen Safety

A safe kitchen is a fun kitchen! Always start your recipes with clean hands, surfaces, and tools. Wash your hands and any tools you may use in future steps of a recipe, especially when handling raw meat. Make sure you have an adult nearby to help you with any task you don't feel comfortable doing, such as cutting vegetables or carrying hot pans.

ALLERGY ALERTS AND TIPS

Have other food allergies? No problem.
Check out the list at the end of each recipe
for substitutions for other common allergens.
Look out for other cool tips and ideas too!

CONVERSIONS

1/4 teaspoon	1.25 grams or milliliters
1/2 teaspoon	2.5 g or mL
1 teaspoon	5 g or mL
1 tablespoon	15 g or mL
1/4 cup	57 g (dry) or 60 mL (liquid)
1/3 cup	75 g (dry) or 80 mL (liquid)
1/2 cup	114 g (dry) or 125 mL (liquid)
2/3 cup	150 g (dry) or 160 mL (liquid)
3/4 cup	170 g (dry) or 175 mL (liquid)
1 cup	227 g (dry) or 240 mL (liquid)
1 quart	950 mL

Fahrenheit (°F)	Celsius (°C)
325°	160°
350°	180°
375°	190°
400°	200°
425°	220°
450°	230°

BAKED FRENCH TOAST
WITH HOMEMADE BLUEBERRY SAUCE

You've probably heard that breakfast is the most important meal of the day. But what do you do when so many breakfast foods include dairy? Perfect for a weekend breakfast, this sweet, dairy-free treat served with a warm fruit topping will taste like dessert.

Prep Time: 8 hours 10 minutes
(8 hours inactive)

Cook Time: 40 minutes

Serves 4

Ingredients

1 cup almond milk, plain

3 eggs

1 teaspoon vanilla extract

¼ teaspoon cinnamon

¼ teaspoon nutmeg

oil, such as vegetable oil

8 slices thick-sliced sandwich bread

Blueberry Sauce

1 cup blueberries

½ cup pure maple syrup

¼ cup lemon or orange juice

½ teaspoon arrowroot powder

Tools

large mixing bowl

measuring cups/spoons

whisk

8 x 8-inch (20 x 20-cm) baking dish

aluminum foil

small saucepan

Allergen Alert!

Swap rice milk for the
almond milk if you need to
avoid both dairy and tree nuts.

Trade plain sandwich bread
for wheat-free bread if
you're allergic to wheat.

Skip the eggs if you have an egg
allergy. You won't miss them!

1. Add the almond milk, eggs, vanilla, cinnamon, and nutmeg to a large mixing bowl.

2. Whisk until the eggs and almond milk are mixed well. Set aside.

3. Grease the baking dish by rubbing some oil on the bottom and sides of the dish.

4. Tear the bread slices into 2-inch (5.1-cm) chunks and place in the baking dish.

5. Pour the egg/almond milk mixture over the top of the bread. It's OK if not all the bread is covered. When the bread sits in the refrigerator, it will soak up the mixture.

6. Cover the dish with aluminum foil and refrigerate overnight.

7. Preheat oven to 350°F to bake.

8. Leave aluminum foil on the dish and place in oven. Bake for 20 minutes. Remove foil carefully and bake an additional 20 minutes.

9. Make your sauce while the French toast bakes. Combine blueberries, maple syrup, and juice in a small saucepan.

10. Place mixture on burner over medium-high heat until it begins to bubble.

11. Turn the heat down to medium and add the arrowroot powder.

12. Allow sauce to simmer for about five minutes and then remove from burner.

13. Spoon out a portion of the French toast bake onto a plate and top with blueberry sauce. Enjoy!

PEACHES 'N CINNAMON OVERNIGHT OATMEAL

Oatmeal is one of many breakfast foods made with milk. Fortunately, almond milk is a great substitute that steers clear of dairy. Mix the ingredients and stow away in the refrigerator the night before for a grab-and-go breakfast you don't have to cook!

Prep Time: 10 minutes

Cook Time: 8 hours (inactive)

Serves 4

Ingredients

2 peaches

2 cups rolled oats

2 cups almond milk

½ teaspoon cinnamon

2 tablespoons pure maple syrup

Tools

cutting board

chef's knife

mixing bowl

measuring cups/spoons

mixing spoon

4 — 1 ½ cup food containers with lids

1. Using the knife and cutting board, slice the peaches. Place the peaches in the mixing bowl.

2. Add oats, almond milk, cinnamon, and maple syrup to the bowl, and mix to combine.

3. Spoon the mixture evenly into the four containers and cover with lids.

4. Place in refrigerator overnight.

5. Enjoy for breakfast the next day!

CHEF'S TIP

Keep your cutting board from moving by placing a damp paper towel underneath it. This will keep your cutting surface sturdy and stable!

BREAKFAST
PIZZA SCRAMBLE

Pizza for breakfast? With a few twists to the ingredient list, you can forego the milk and cheese. You'll want to set your alarm clock early for this spin on a classic that's easy to make and tasty to eat!

Prep Time: 10 minutes

Cook Time: 10 minutes

Serves 4

Ingredients

4 slices sandwich bread

2 eggs

1 tablespoon water

2 teaspoons oil

¼ cup pizza sauce or tomato sauce

4 tablespoons nutritional yeast

Tools

toaster

mixing bowl

whisk

non-stick skillet

spatula

large baking sheet

Allergen Alert!

Wheat-free bread can take the place of regular sandwich bread in this recipe.

Switch out scrambled eggs with chopped avocado if you have an egg allergy.

1. Preheat the oven broiler on high.

2. Toast the slices of bread in toaster until golden brown. Set aside.

3. Crack the eggs into a mixing bowl and add the water. Whisk until the yolks and whites are blended. Set aside.

4. Heat the oil over a burner on medium heat in a non-stick skillet.

5. Add the eggs. Stir with spatula until cooked and liquid is absorbed. Remove from heat.

6. Spread the pizza or tomato sauce on the toasted bread slices.

7. Arrange the scrambled eggs evenly on top of the sauce.

8. Sprinkle tablespoon nutritional yeast over the eggs on each piece of toast.

9. Arrange toasts on a large baking sheet, and place in oven for about three minutes.

10. Remove from oven and serve hot.

CHEF'S TIP

Pump up your protein intake by adding some of your favorite allergen-free meat to your scramble!

CHICKEN AND WILD RICE
SOUP

Craving a creamy comfort food? Some soups use milk to create a smooth, creamy texture. Coconut milk takes the place of dairy in this creamy concoction. Perfect on a cool fall day, this chicken and wild rice soup will warm you right up.

Prep Time: 10 minutes

Cook Time: 1 hour

Serves 4

Ingredients

1 onion

2 carrots

1 tablespoon oil

4 cups chicken broth

1 pound (16 ounces) skinless, boneless chicken thighs

1 cup wild rice/brown rice mix

1 teaspoon dried thyme

1 cup coconut milk

salt and pepper

Tools

cutting board

chef's knife

vegetable peeler

large pot

measuring cups/spoons

1. Peel and and chop the onion.

2. Peel the carrots using a vegetable peeler, then slice each carrot.

3. Add the oil, onion, and carrots in a large pot over medium heat. Cook for about five minutes, or until the vegetables start to soften.

4. Add the chicken broth and bring to a simmer.

5. Cut the chicken thighs into 1-inch (2.5-cm) cubes while the broth is warming.

6. Add the chicken to the bubbling broth, and cook for 10 minutes.

7. Pour the rice mix and thyme into the pot and reduce the heat to medium-low. Cook for about 45 minutes, stirring occasionally.

8. Add the coconut milk and simmer for five minutes, until thickened.

9. Season the soup with salt and pepper a pinch at a time until seasoned to your liking.

10. Serve hot in bowls.

CHEF'S TIP

Cutting an onion can make your eyes tear up. To avoid irritating your peepers, pop the onion in the freezer for about 10 minutes before chopping.

RANCH CHICKEN BITES

Did you know that fried chicken is often made with buttermilk? Acids in the buttermilk break down the chicken to make it juicy and tender. But don't take chicken strips off the menu yet! The acids in yogurt work the same way. Crispy on the outside, juicy on the inside, these chicken strips with dipping sauce are sure to please.

Prep Time: 20 minutes

Cook Time: 20 minutes

Serves 4

Ingredients

2 cups coconut milk yogurt

1 tablespoon dried parsley

2 teaspoons dried dill

1 teaspoon garlic powder

1 teaspoon onion powder

1 teaspoon lemon juice

½ teaspoon salt

½ teaspoon ground black pepper

2 boneless, skinless chicken breasts

salt and pepper

2 cups crispy corn hexagon cereal

¼ cup olive oil

Tools

measuring cups/spoons

mixing bowls

non-wooden spoon

plastic wrap

cutting board

chef's knife

gallon-size zip-top bag

rolling pin

plate

large skillet

spatula or tongs

Allergen Alert!

If you are allergic to wheat, make sure
your corn cereal is certified wheat-free.

1. Combine the coconut milk yogurt, parsley, dill, garlic powder, onion powder, lemon juice, salt, and pepper in a mixing bowl. Stir well with a spoon and set aside.

2. Cut each of the chicken breasts into 4 equal strips (8 total), and sprinkle lightly with salt and pepper on both sides.

3. Separate 1 cup of the yogurt mix and place in a second mixing bowl.

4. Add chicken to one of the bowls and stir to coat.

5. Cover the other bowl of yogurt mix with plastic wrap and place in refrigerator until later.

6. Pour the corn cereal into the zip-top bag and seal. Set the bag on a counter or surface. Gently crush the cereal by tapping the bag with the rolling pin, until the cereal resembles breadcrumbs. Pour the crushed cereal onto a plate.

7. Set a large skillet on a burner on medium heat. Add the oil.

8. Roll each piece of chicken around in the crumbs, until covered.

9. Place the chicken in the skillet, avoiding splatters. Cook for about five minutes per side or until golden brown on the outside and no longer pink inside.

10. Remove chicken from skillet and place on a plate lined with paper towels to soak up excess oil.

11. Serve hot with remaining yogurt dipping sauce.

15

CREAMY MASHED
POTATOES

Mashed potatoes get their smooth, creamy texture from butter and cream or milk. That's a lot of dairy products to avoid, but don't despair! Grab some spuds and get started on this alternate recipe that is even better than the original!

Prep Time: 10 minutes

Cook Time: 25 minutes

Serves 4

Ingredients

1 ½ pounds (24 oz) Yukon gold potatoes, plus water and salt for cooking

¼ cup chicken broth

¼ cup rice milk

3 tablespoons olive oil

½ teaspoon salt

½ teaspoon ground black pepper

Tools

vegetable peeler

cutting board

chef's knife

large pot

measuring cups/spoons

small saucepan

colander

potato masher

Allergen Alert!

If you follow a soy-free diet, check the ingredients list on the broth to make sure it is certified soy-free.

1. Clean potatoes under running water and peel using a vegetable peeler.

2. Cut into 2-inch (5.1-cm) cubes and place in a large pot.

3. Add enough water to cover the potatoes in the pot. Add 1 tablespoon salt.

4. Place pot on a burner set to medium-high and bring to a boil. Once boiling, turn the heat down to simmer. Cook for 20 minutes or until tender.

5. Place the chicken broth, rice milk, olive oil, salt, and pepper in a small saucepan. Cook over medium heat until it barely bubbles. Remove from heat and set aside.

6. Drain the potatoes and return them to the pot. Pour about half of the warm rice milk/broth mixture over the potatoes.

7. Use a potato masher to gently mash the potatoes. Add more liquid a little at a time until potatoes are fluffy.

8. Taste for seasoning. If they need a little more salt, add a pinch at a time.

9. Serve hot with Swedish Meatballs or alongside any of your favorite dinnertime main courses.

SWEDISH MEATBALLS

One of Scandinavia's prized dishes gets its fame for soft and tender meatballs smothered in a cream sauce. You can re-create this savory entrée without the cream! This delicious, comforting dish tastes great on top of the Creamy Mashed Potatoes.

Prep Time: 30 minutes

Cook Time: 30 minutes

Serves 4

Ingredients

Meatballs

1 small onion

1 pound (16 oz) ground pork

1 teaspoon salt

½ teaspoon pepper

¼ teaspoon ground nutmeg

¼ teaspoon ground cardamom

Sauce

2 cups beef broth

½ cup coconut cream

2 tablespoons arrowroot powder

salt and pepper, to taste

Tools

large baking sheet

parchment paper

cutting board

chef's knife

box grater

large mixing bowl

measuring spoons/cups

large skillet

whisk

Allergen Alert!

If you follow a soy-free diet, check the ingredients list on the beef broth to make sure it is certified free of soy.

1. Preheat oven to 375°F. Line a large baking sheet with parchment paper and set aside.

2. Cut the onion in half and peel the skin off using the cutting board and chef's knife. Then grate it using the side of the box grater with the smallest holes.

3. Place grated onion in the large mixing bowl and set aside.

4. Add the pork, salt, pepper, nutmeg, and cardamom to the bowl.

5. Squish the mixture with your hands until everything is mixed well.

6. Use a spoon to roll meatballs. Evenly scoop out portions (about 2 tablespoons each) of the meat mixture, and roll between palms.

7. Place the meatballs on the baking sheet ½ inch (1.3 cm) apart. Bake in the oven for about 20 minutes or until no longer pink inside.

8. Make the sauce while the meatballs bake. Combine the beef broth, coconut cream, and arrowroot powder in a large skillet. Whisk ingredients quickly to dissolve.

9. Bring mixture to a low simmer over medium heat until thickened slightly.

10. Add the meatballs to the skillet with the sauce when they are done and stir well. Add salt and pepper a pinch at a time until seasoned to your liking.

11. Serve hot. This dish also tastes great on top of the Creamy Mashed Potatoes. Add a little sauce to top it off.

TACO SALAD

Head south of the border for this dairy-free delight! Crispy and fresh, this Mexican-inspired salad avoids the cheese and sour cream but adds many tantalizing ingredients.

Prep Time: 45 minutes (30 minutes inactive)

Cook Time: 20 minutes

Serves 4

Ingredients

2 boneless, skinless chicken breasts

2 tablespoons olive oil

1 tablespoon lime juice

1 tablespoon ground cumin

2 tablespoons chili powder

1 teaspoon dried oregano

½ teaspoon salt

½ teaspoon ground black pepper

1 10-ounce bag chopped romaine lettuce

2 ripe tomatoes

1 small red onion, peeled

1 10-ounce can corn, drained

1 cup corn tortilla strips

Avocado Dressing

2 ripe avocados

1 8-ounce can full-fat coconut milk

2 tablespoons lime juice

1 teaspoon dried dill

1 teaspoon garlic powder

1 teaspoon dried thyme

½ teaspoon salt

½ teaspoon ground black pepper

Tools

2 cutting boards, one for raw chicken and one for vegetables

chef's knife

2 large mixing bowls

measuring spoons

whisk

plastic wrap

blender

large skillet

tongs

1. Cut the pieces of chicken into 1-inch (2.5-cm) chunks and set aside.

2. Whisk together the oil, lime juice, cumin, chili powder, oregano, salt, and pepper in one large mixing bowl until blended.

3. Add the chicken, and stir to coat. Cover with plastic wrap and allow chicken to marinate for 30 minutes.

4. Make the avocado cream dressing while the chicken marinates. Ask an adult to help you cut the avocados in half and remove the pits. Scoop out the pulp and place in a blender with remaining dressing ingredients.

5. Blend on high until consistency is thin, adding water 1 tablespoon at a time, if necessary.

6. Chop tomatoes and onion and set aside.

7. When the chicken is done marinating, heat a large skillet over a burner set to medium.

8. Add the chicken and marinade to the skillet. Stir occasionally while the meat cooks, about seven minutes, or until no longer pink.

9. Assemble the salad in the second large mixing bowl. Add the lettuce, tomatoes, onion, corn, and chicken. Drizzle the avocado dressing lightly over the salad and toss gently with tongs to mix. Top with the tortilla strips and serve with more avocado cream dressing, if desired.

Allergens Eradicated!

No major food allergens found here!

CREAMY PASTA CARBONARA

Traditionally, this dish is made with both cream and eggs. But you won't be missing them at all with this flavorful pasta bowl.

Prep Time: 10 minutes

Cook Time: 20 minutes

Serves 4

Ingredients

4 slices thick-sliced bacon

1 small onion

1 tablespoons olive oil

8 ounces uncooked spaghetti pasta, plus water and salt for cooking

1 ½ cups plain rice milk

3 teaspoons arrowroot powder

1 teaspoon garlic powder

1 cup frozen peas

2 tablespoons nutritional yeast

salt and pepper

Tools

cutting board

chef's knife

large skillet

measuring spoons/cups

large pot

colander

whisk

tongs

Allergen Alert!

If you have a wheat allergy, be aware of your bacon! Make sure the label reads certified gluten-free.

You should also swap the semolina pasta with wheat-free pasta if you are allergic to wheat.

1. Carefully cut the bacon into ½-inch (1.3-cm) pieces using a cutting board and chef's knife. Place bacon pieces in a large skillet.

2. Peel and chop the onion and add to the skillet along with the olive oil.

3. Place skillet with bacon, onion, and olive oil onto a burner set to medium heat. Slowly cook until the bacon is crisp and onions tender. Look out for splatters! Remove from heat when done.

4. Ask an adult to help you drain the fat from the skillet, and set aside.

5. Fill a large pot ¾ full of water and add 1 tablespoon salt. Put the pot on a burner over high heat until it begins to boil.

6. Reduce the heat and add the pasta, cooking according to package directions until done. Drain and set aside.

7. Place the skillet with the bacon and onions back on a burner on medium-high heat.

8. Add rice milk, arrowroot powder, and garlic powder to the pan. Whisk quickly to dissolve powders.

9. When the liquid starts to bubble, reduce the heat to medium and continue whisking until it thickens. Add more arrowroot powder, 1 teaspoon at a time for more thickness.

10. Add the drained pasta, frozen peas, and nutritional yeast to the skillet and toss gently with tongs. Taste sauce, and add salt and pepper as needed, a pinch at a time.

11. Serve hot with extra nutritional yeast on the side to sprinkle on top.

NO-CHEESE
VEGGIE DIP

You'd never guess this cheese sauce doesn't actually have cheese. Ooey-gooey and so delicious—it makes all vegetables taste good!

Prep Time: 15 minutes

Makes 1 cup

Ingredients

2 tablespoons non-dairy buttery
   spread

1 tablespoon all-purpose flour

¾ cup rice milk

½ cup nutritional yeast

1 teaspoon mustard powder

1 teaspoon salt

½ teaspoon black pepper

Tools

measuring cups/spoons

medium skillet

whisk

Allergen Alert!

Make sure you use a wheat-free
flour mixture if you have a wheat allergy.

1. Melt the buttery spread in a medium-sized skillet on a burner set to medium-high heat.

2. Add the flour and whisk until the mixture resembles wet sand.

3. Pour in the milk, whisking quickly at the same time.

4. When the mixture begins to bubble, turn the heat down to medium.

5. Add the nutritional yeast, mustard powder, salt, and pepper and whisk again to combine.

6. Allow the sauce to cook for about five minutes, or until it thickens slightly. If it is too runny, add flour 1 teaspoon at a time until it thickens to your desired thickness.

7. Remove from heat and serve hot to dip in with raw cut vegetables.

CHEF'S TIP

This dip can also be drizzled on top of your
favorite cooked veggies. You can even stir
in a few tablespoons with cooked pasta for
another favorite—mac and cheese!

BANANA ICE CREAM

Ice cream is a dessert loaded with dairy.
But you can still go cold and creamy with
a simple banana creation. You only need
two ingredients to make this imitation
ice cream on a hot summer day!

Prep Time: 2 hours and 10 minutes
(2 hours inactive)

Serves 4

Ingredients

4 very ripe bananas

½ teaspoon vanilla extract

Tools

cutting board

butter knife

freezer-safe zip-top bag

food processor or blender

Allergens Eradicated!

No major food allergens found here!

1. Peel the bananas and slice into 1-inch (2.5-cm) thick rounds on a cutting board.

2. Put the banana rounds into a zip top bag and place in a freezer for at least two hours.

3. Add the frozen bananas and vanilla extract to a food processor or blender. Use the pulse button to chop the bananas into chunks.

4. Set the food processor or blender on high speed. Closely watch the bananas blend until they have a consistency like soft-serve ice cream. It can take several minutes.

5. Serve immediately, or freeze in an airtight, freezer-safe container and keep for up to one week.

CHEF'S TIP

Add mix-ins such as strawberries, raspberries, mangoes, or allergen-free chocolate to your ice cream!

HOT CHOCOLATE
WITH WHIPPED CREAM

No dairy, no problem. You can still warm up on a cold winter's evening with a hot mug of this chocolatey delight!

Prep Time: 8 hours 10 minutes
(8 hours inactive)

Cook Time: 5 minutes

Serves 4

Ingredients

Coconut Whipped Cream

1 8-ounce can coconut cream

½ cup confectioner's sugar

½ teaspoon vanilla extract

Hot Chocolate

1 quart rice milk or
  unsweetened almond milk

½ cup semisweet cocoa powder

½ cup pure honey

2 teaspoons vanilla extract

Tools

can opener

medium mixing bowl

electric hand mixer with
  whisk attachment

measuring cups/spoons

large saucepan

spoon

Allergen Alert!

If you have a tree nut allergy, make sure
your chocolate is certified nut-free.

1. Place the can of coconut cream in the refrigerator overnight before whipping.

2. Add the cream to a medium-sized mixing bowl.

3. Using the electric hand mixer on high, whip the coconut cream until light and fluffy.

4. Add the confectioner's sugar and vanilla extract. Whip on high for another 30 seconds until combined. Place finished cream in refrigerator.

5. Make the hot chocolate while the whipped cream chills. Combine all the hot chocolate ingredients in a large saucepan and stir well.

6. Place over a burner on medium heat. Slowly heat the liquid to avoid burning the chocolate. When it just begins to bubble, it's ready.

7. Pour hot chocolate into mugs and top with a dollop of coconut whipped cream.

8. Store leftover coconut cream in an airtight container in refrigerator for up to one week.

BERRY NUTRITIOUS SMOOTHIE

Who says you need milk to make a super thick shake? With a blender and some fruity flavors, you can turn your kitchen into a smoothie stand to make this sweet treat that's easy to make and take with you!

Prep Time: 5 minutes

Makes 1 smoothie

Ingredients

1 cup frozen mixed berries

1 banana

¾ cup rice milk

2 tablespoons honey

½ teaspoon vanilla extract

Tools

measuring cups/spoons

blender

Allergens Eradicated!

No major food allergens found here!

1. Combine the frozen berries, banana, rice milk, honey, and vanilla extract in the pitcher of a blender.

2. Pulse 5–6 times to break up the chunks, and then turn to high until smooth.

3. Serve in a glass and enjoy immediately.

For a super thick smoothie, add a handful of ice cubes to the blender.

GLOSSARY

assemble—to put all the parts of something together

blend—to mix together, sometimes using a blender

boil—to heat until large bubbles form on top of a liquid; the boiling point for water is 212°F (100°C)

concoction—a mixture of different things

consume—to eat or drink something

dissolve—to incorporate a solid food into a liquid by melting or stirring

drizzle—to let a substance fall in small drops

mash—to smash a soft food into a lumpy mixture

pit—the single central seed or stone of certain fruits

pulp—the soft juicy or fleshy part of a fruit or vegetable

simmer—to keep just below boiling when cooking or heating

slice—to cut into thin pieces with a knife

whisk—to stir a mixture rapidly until it's smooth

READ MORE

Ainsworth, Mark. *The Young Chef: Recipes and Techniques for Kids Who Love to Cook.* Boston: Houghton Mifflin Harcourt, 2016.

Clark, Pamela. *Allergy-free Cooking for Kids.* New York: Sterling Epicure, 2014.

Cook, Deanna F. *Cooking Class: 57 Fun Recipes Kids will Love to Make (and Eat!).* North Adams, MA: Storey Publishing, 2015.

INTERNET SITES

Use FactHound to find Internet sites related to this book. All of the sites on FactHound have been researched by our staff.

Here's all you do:

Visit *www.facthound.com*

Type in this code: 9781491480533